THE HISTORY CHANNEL® PRESENTS

TACTICAL TO PRACTICAL™

FLASH, BOOM, BLAST!

AMAZING INVENTIONS FROM THE WAR FRONT!

Read all the books in

THE HISTORY CHANNEL® PRESENTS
TACTICAL TO PRACTICAL™

FLASH, BOOM, BLAST!

AMAZING INVENTIONS FROM THE WAR FRONT!

By Laurie Calkhoven

SCHOLASTIC INC.
New York   Toronto   London   Auckland   Sydney
Mexico City   New Delhi   Hong Kong   Buenos Aires

ISBN 0-439-68357-2

Cover designed by Louise Bova
Interior designed by Dawn Adelman

12 11 10 9 8 7 6 5 4 3 2 1   4 5 6 7 8/0

Printed in the U.S.A.
First printing, November 2004

CONTENTS

THE HISTORY CHANNEL® PRESENTS

TACTICAL TO PRACTICAL™

FLASH, BOOM, BLAST!

AMAZING INVENTIONS FROM THE WAR FRONT!

INTRODUCTION

You're on a battlefield at night. Missiles explode on the horizon. You've joined your fellow U.S. soldiers on the front lines and bear down on the enemy.

Your radio beeps. You get the order – a U.S. pilot has been shot down behind enemy lines. Your mission? Search and rescue.

You quickly jump into your desert patrol vehicle along with two crew members and race into enemy territory. Night-vision goggles help you to see as clearly as you would during the day. Pictures taken by the Predator drone let you know exactly where the enemy troops are hiding. The GPS (Global Positioning System) leads you into enemy territory.

Deep inside enemy territory, you spot the pilot. He appears to be injured, and the enemy is closing in! Can you get there first?

You get in fast, scoop him up, and get out again before the enemy even knows you were there. But there's a 50-caliber machine gun mounted on your DPV (Desert Patrol Vehicle) just in case. If necessary, you and your crew are ready to fight.

Your first priority is getting that injured pilot medical care. You race back toward the front lines under the cloak of darkness. As you approach U.S. troops, their Blue Force Tracking system tells them that you're friend, not foe. And you slip safely back across the line of fire — mission accomplished.

The injured pilot will be lifted out by helicopter and will live to fly again.

In the United States military, these stories are real.

When you're fighting for your life, every second counts. Every piece of military equipment needs to be the best. And it needs to be more powerful and more advanced than the enemy's.

Maybe that's why the military keeps coming up

with the high-tech inventions that help make the United States fighting force the best in the world. What's amazing is how often military technology becomes stuff we use in everyday life.

The tactical becomes practical!

Working with The History Channel®, we've uncovered some of the military's greatest and most daring innovations: tactical inventions that also play a practical role in civilian life — like global positioning satellites that can pinpoint military targets on the battlefield and tell us to turn left at the corner! And planes that can fly without a

pilot for tricky spy missions or film otherwise impossible-to-get camera shots for Hollywood blockbuster movies.

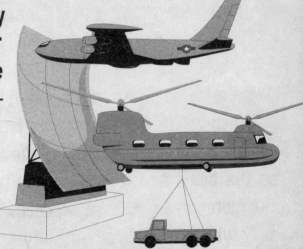

Tactical to practical: developed for tactical advantage, declassified for practical use.

1

AMAZING FLYING MACHINES

It's been just over one hundred years since the Wright brothers invented their flying machine. Since then, we've flown to the moon, broken the sound barrier, and invented air-planes that can take off on water or land. There are even planes that can fly without a pilot!

UAVS: PLANES WITHOUT PILOTS

Tactical: Unmanned aerial vehicles (UAVs) fly dangerous missions, keeping pilots safe.

Practical: Camera-carrying UAVs make movie magic by going places no camera has gone before.

THE KETTERING BUG

Since the earliest days of flight, people have imagined that unmanned aircraft could be used to blast the bad guys while keeping pilots out of harm's way.

In 1918, Orville Wright collaborated with Charles Kettering and invented the world's first cruise missile — the Kettering Aerial Torpedo (nicknamed the "Bug").

Charles Kettering's Bug, a small plane with a wingspan of about 15 feet and 180 pounds of explosives on board, was designed to hit a target 50 miles away. After it was airborne for a preset length of time, the Bug shut down its engine and disconnected its wings. When it plunged to Earth, the explosives detonated on impact.

The Bug did its job in early test runs, but World War I was over before the army could try its new

Declassified Quiz:

Charles F. Kettering is best known for which invention?

a. the electric self-starter for automobiles
b. the electric cash register
c. the spark plug
d. four-wheel brakes

Answer: All of the above! Charles Kettering was a coholder of more than 140 patents!

flying bomb against the enemy. Fewer than 50 Bugs had been built when Germany surrendered. None was ever used in combat.

WORLD WAR II DRONES

With World War II looming, UAVs (also known as drones) improved dramatically. The military developed new uses, switching their tactical applications from offensive to defensive.

The Radioplane drone — a small radio-controlled plane with a wingspan of about 12 feet and a maximum speed of 85 miles per hour — turned out to be just what the army needed to train antiaircraft gunners.

In target practice, Radioplanes looked like full-size aircraft, sounded like full-size aircraft, and flew attack maneuvers like full-size aircraft. And they got shot down just like full-size aircraft!

They were the first UAVs, and the military ordered them by the thousands to train the troops.

PREPARE FOR TAKEOFF

Let's fast-forward 50 years to the biggest and fastest UAV — the Global Hawk. The Hawk is a high-altitude reconnaissance UAV that can take incredible pictures while flying more than 10 miles up in the sky. From half a world away, the

Global Hawk sends back images of enemy troop movements to battlefield commanders, giving them the information they need to win a war as quickly as possible. All before the enemy has time to say "cheese."

CONFIDENTIAL

CIVILIAN UAVS

You'll be amazed at how this technology has crossed over to the civilian side. Camera-equipped UAVs film impossible-to-get shots for Hollywood blockbuster movies, music videos, and commercials — all without risking a pilot's life!

SECRETS DECLASSIFIED

The Global Hawk has a wingspan of just over 116 feet and a maximum speed of 454 miles per hour!

Coptervision, a company in California, has a fleet of eight miniature remote-controlled helicopters equipped with cameras that not only pan and tilt (rotate horizontally and vertically to keep an object in the picture), but can even roll, too. These helicopter cameras can go places too dangerous for a full-size helicopter.

FROM THE FALCONER TO THE PREDATOR

Like Hollywood, the military pushes the boundaries of technology to get must-have camera shots. In the 1950s, the Army Signal Corps set its sights on unmanned aerial surveillance. The Falconer and other camera-equipped drones were invented to film enemy troops and their movements.

At that time, you had to get the drone back and develop the film in order to see the pictures. If the drone finished its mission but crashed on the way home, the military was left with nothing. Today, the military can see pictures half a second after the drone takes them!

By the end of the 1990s, the military relied more and more on surveillance UAVs like the Predator to send target positions back to military command centers in real time. But, until recently, pilots and attack aircraft still had to be called in to finish the job.

In battle, every second counts. So what did the military do? They armed the UAVs.

In 2002, U.S. forces turned up the heat on enemies by turning the Predator into a lethal weapon. Using the pictures the Predator sends back to a command center, a soldier can press a button from thousands of miles away to take out a target.

MODEL UAVS

Serious hobbyists can build and fly smaller UAVs at speeds of more than 200 miles per hour! Some even come with cameras that will give you your own eye in the sky. Now, not only can you be a secret agent (want to check out the other team's football plays?), but you can also star in your own mission impossible.

THE POINTER

It's not only on the practical side that UAVs are

SECRETS DECLASSIFIED

The Predator, a medium-altitude UAV, flew more than 600 missions in Bosnia and has since been used in Operation Desert Storm and Operation Iraqi Freedom.

getting smaller. In Afghanistan and Operation Iraqi Freedom, one of the most advanced tools used by Special Operations teams is the Pointer, a 10-pound UAV with an on-board camera.

The Pointer is so easy to use that one soldier can set it up and let it fly. The pictures it relays back can be viewed in seconds, giving soldiers an aerial view of any enemies that might be hiding over the next ridge or behind a nearby building.

SECRETS DECLASSIFIED

Japanese farmers use the UAVs to plant rice — saving lots of time and money.

In the future, UAVs will range in size from the Predator down to something that's small enough to fly out of a soldier's hand and let him know what's hiding around the next corner.

Is it possible that someday the military won't need human pilots at all? Only time will tell.

HELIOS

The highest-flying and weirdest-looking UAV of them all is the Helios! With a wingspan longer than the 747's, it might look like a flock of migrating birds at first glance. But this UAV (which weighs less than a small car) has been flown by NASA up to 100,000 feet, and because it's powered by the sun, it can be flown for months at a time.

Though it's still experimental, the Helios could one day be used as a communications platform to speed up your Internet connection! It could also monitor weather, track hurricanes, and give rescue workers information about disaster sites (such as forest fires, mud slides, floods, and earthquakes).

The future looks promising for UAVs as they take over more and more of the dull, dirty, and dangerous work done by manned aircraft. UAVs are being developed to detect chemical and biological weapons, and even to fly combat missions.

Who knows, maybe one day you'll fly from New York to California in a plane without a pilot!

HELICOPTERS – TANKS IN THE SKY

Tactical: Helicopters are a fearsome force on the battlefield.

Practical: Helicopters take civilians anywhere they want to go.

Riding in helicopters is a lot of fun, but for the military, aircraft that can hover in the air—as well as take off and land vertically—are important parts of combat strategy.

Long before helicopters saw action on the battlefield, they were just trying to get off the ground. Inventors couldn't even think about launching these dream machines into the air until a powerful engine was built in

the late nineteenth century. In 1907, a French inventor named Paul Cornu lifted a twin-rotored helicopter into the air without any assistance for the first time.

THE FLYING OCTOPUS

Once the civilian side got helicopters up into the air, the military paid attention. In 1922, the U.S. Army got its first helicopter — the Flying Octopus. Then in World War II, helicopters ferried critical parts from ships to B-29 bomber squadrons on islands in the Pacific. But it wasn't until the Vietnam War that helicopters became a fighting force to be reckoned with.

ATTACK HELICOPTERS

Before Vietnam, helicopter power was limited. Then the military got its first attack helicopter — the Bell Cobra.

Declassified Quiz:

What's the Super Cobra's nickname?
a. Attack Bird
b. Snake
c. Bird of Prey

Answer: b. Marines call the Super Cobra "Snake" after its deadly namesake.

The Bell Cobra flew more than one million flying hours in Vietnam. It also revolutionized the army's war tactics. Not only did it give fire support to troops on the ground, the Cobra moved soldiers in and out of combat zones and evacuated wounded soldiers from the battlefield super quickly. The Cobra could go places fixed-wing airplanes could never go.

Today's Super Cobra — complete with night vision and an arsenal of lethal weapons — is the war bird relied on by the U.S. Marines.

The army's attack helicopter is the Apache — the most lethal helicopter in the world. It can operate day or night and in any kind of weather.

It's mobile, agile, and equipped for combat. During the Persian Gulf War, the Apache had what it took to put the enemy on the run.

HELICOPTERS HELPING PEOPLE

Helicopters are not only critical in every branch of the military; they changed the way we get around the world. More than three million people have flown above, around, and down into the Grand Canyon in helicopters. But more important is the use of helicopters for emergency medical transport, search-and-rescue missions, police services, and news and traffic reporting. Helicopters have done everything from amazing us at air shows to rescuing people off the decks of sinking ships.

SPECIAL-DUTY PLANES

Tactical: Special-duty aircraft land where normal planes can't.

Practical: Rugged planes and pilots conquer the wilderness of Alaska.

Some can land on water; others can land on a dime. Special-duty airplanes are built to go just about anywhere.

SEAPLANES

There is a lot more water than land on the surface of the Earth. That's why aviation pioneers wanted to find a way to take off and land on water. The first type of "go anywhere" plane was the seaplane.

A man named Glenn Curtiss invented the first American seaplane in 1911 and later built them for military use. In the 1930s, his Curtiss Scout observation plane was catapulted from warships. The seaplane then radioed back enemy positions before it returned to land alongside the ship and was hauled aboard by crane.

During World War II, the PBY-5A Catalina flying boat became the most popular military seaplane ever built. One of the first airplanes to carry radar, it was used for both reconnaissance and rescue.

Not only did the Catalina locate the German battleship *Bismarck* in the Atlantic Ocean in 1941, a Catalina spotted the Japanese fleet during the opening phase of the Battle of Midway — a turn-

SECRETS DECLASSIFIED

The Battle of Midway was fought in June 1942 near the Midway Islands. The U.S. victory over the Japanese ended a major Japanese attempt to capture the Midway Islands as a possible first step to an invasion of Hawaii.

ing point for the United States in the war.

By 1947, the Grumman Albatross — 60 feet long and 80 feet across the wingspan — had become a mainstay of the navy and the air force, where it was used for military patrols and air-sea rescue missions in Alaska and Antarctica. Today, the Albatross hauls cargo and tourists across the Alaskan wilderness.

THE SPRUCE GOOSE

During World War II, the military had a critical need to transport troops across the Atlantic and keep them safe from deadly German submarines. Howard Hughes designed the largest seaplane ever built: the Spruce Goose. Wider than the length of a football field, it had eight engines and could hold up to 700 troops.

Most people didn't believe that such a humongous plane could actually fly. But in 1947, during what was supposed to be a taxi test, Hughes surprised everyone by flying the plane for 60 seconds. While the plane was too late for wartime application, its flight was one of the most famous in aviation history.

SHORT TAKEOFF AND LANDING PLANES

Though big planes like the Spruce Goose turned out to be pretty impractical as a form of transportation, one of the other innovations of World War II is still with us today.

Short takeoff and landing aircraft (STOL's) planes were developed by the military in World War II to get troops and equipment to areas with short landing strips. STOL planes are still used by bush pilots and commuter airlines today to get in and out of tight spaces in the wild. Most bush planes need only about 55 yards to come to a full stop. Others like the Mountain Goat needs only 40!

Declassified Quiz:

After its test flight, what did Howard Hughes do with his 23-million-dollar seaplane?

a. put it back in the hangar and never flew it again
b. started his own commercial airline
c. used it for the first trans-Atlantic flight

Answer: The Spruce Goose never flew again.

VERTICAL TAKEOFF AND LANDING AIRCRAFT

What about when 40 yards isn't short enough? The air force and NASA have been testing vertical takeoff and landing (VTOL's) planes for almost 50 years. These aircraft have to combine the versatility of a helicopter with the speed of a plane.

The V-22 Osprey takes off and lands like a helicopter, but once it's airborne, it's capable of the same high-speed, high-altitude flight as an airplane. A civilian version is in development for use in search-and-rescue operations and may be airborne as early as 2007.

So what will planes look like in the future? With small aircraft that need only short runways or no runway at all, maybe one day we'll fly over traffic rather than get stuck in it. One thing's for sure, the U.S. military will continue to lead the world in inventing and developing the world's fiercest and fastest flying machines.

2

TACTICAL COMBAT, PRACTICAL CRIME FIGHTING

Spy gear is cool! No wonder Hollywood makes so many movies about it. But in real life, spy gear is all about catching the bad guys and keeping secret agents alive. CIA and FBI agents have been using covert surveillance and high-tech forensic tools for years. Now those same tools are available to cops all over the country.

SPY GEAR

Tactical: Spy craft gives the military powerful tools for secret maneuvers.

Practical: High-tech spy gear traps crooks in their tracks.

Professional spies have to be able to gain access to secret information, steal it, and escape undetected. Their tools? Concealed cameras, secret disguises, and hidden weapons.

CATCHING THE BAD GUYS ON FILM

Using cameras for espionage has been one of the basic tools of spying since photography was invented.

In 1936, a photographer's assistant named Walter Zapp set out to create a lighter, smaller camera — one that had an outstanding lens and was easy to use. Zapp had no idea that his invention would turn out to be one of the most important tools of espionage.

His Minox Subminiature Camera — small enough to be hidden in the palm of his hand — became the world's most widely used spy camera.

Declassified Quiz:

During the Civil War, Union scouts spied on Confederate troop positions with cameras mounted on hot-air balloons. True or false?

Answer: True.

By the end of World War II, cameras got even smaller. They were hidden in seemingly innocent devices — like pens, watches, lighters, and even buttons. Secretly photographing documents and people became easier and easier.

THE COLD WAR

Most espionage methods were invented during a time of fear, under the looming threat of nuclear attack.

When the United States and the Soviet Union raced to be the first to develop nuclear weapons, the Cold War Era began. In 1947, Congress passed the National Security Act and created the Central Intelligence Agency.

The CIA was given the job of conducting secret operations to protect national security. The agency launched a new era in espionage, not to mention an awesome arsenal of spy technology.

Today, the high-powered camera lenses and ultrasensitive microphones once available only to secret agents are used regularly by undercover

SECRETS DECLASSIFIED

The biggest trend in spy technology over the past 50 years has been miniaturization — smaller and smaller cameras, microphones, and other communications devices.

Tony Mendez, the CIA's Chief of Disguise, created a fake Hollywood film production company (complete with employees, scripts, publicity, and real estate) to get U.S. diplomats out of Iran. He was awarded the Intelligence Star for Valor by President Jimmy Carter for single-handedly planning and conducting the escape.

law enforcement officers.

That same kind of equipment is also available to average citizens to protect their property. Want to check on your dog or make sure your cat hasn't gotten into the fish tank when you're away from home? Using cameras with wireless Internet technology makes that as easy as logging on to a computer.

MASTERS OF DISGUISE

Espionage is more than just hidden cameras. Spies have to be experts at hiding their identities. Experts in disguise for the CIA use facial hair, makeup, and wigs to disguise agents so they can penetrate enemy territory. They've even been known to disguise men as women and women as men.

In 1979, when Iranian students took 52 Americans hostage in Iran, CIA disguises made it possible for six U.S. Embassy employees to sneak out of the country.

Believe it or not, these concealment techniques are still in daily use by undercover agents around the world — spies whose lives depend on hiding their identities as well as their weapons.

SECRET WEAPONS

Basically, anything that you can carry can be turned into a weapon by the experts at the CIA.

Ever heard of a lipstick gun? Or a gun hidden in a glove? Those are just a couple of tricks that American spies might have up their sleeves. Gives a whole new meaning to the phrase "point

SECRETS DECLASSIFIED

What happens when a spy doesn't have a weapon? He or she has to be one. Ancient martial arts techniques are incorporated into hand-to-hand combat training for spies and special agents for those risky situations.

and shoot," huh? Ingenuity and imagination contributed to a wide variety of hidden firearms during the Cold War.

SMART DUST

The basic mission of spying is anticipating potential threats and heading them off. New enemies create new challenges. Future spies will rely on devices so small, it will be almost impossible to know they're there.

One new technology is called Smart Dust. Tiny electronic sensors the size of dust particles can be scattered in the air to detect chemical or biological agents. By using minuscule lasers, the sensors are able to transmit information to a base miles away.

Soon these tiny spies could be dropped from planes to measure the weather inside storms, or discover almost anything, anywhere.

Spy craft is a dangerous game of secrets and subterfuge, and future spy gear will have to keep up.

MILITARY CRIME FIGHTING

Tactical: Military police fight crime among the ranks.

Practical: Military technology helps fight crime on the streets.

The police officers on a SWAT (Special Weapons and Tactics) team look as if they're training for war. They are. Many of the tools used by today's peacekeepers were developed by the military. But there's a twist. Military police often use techniques developed by civilian crime fighters to enforce law and order.

MPs move fast, work as a team, and overwhelm the enemy. What do they do if a VIP military escort comes under attack? Or gun-carrying terrorists block the road? They rely on high-speed, evasive driving. And they learned those tricks from civilian police officers, who developed them in hot pursuit of the bad guys.

FORENSIC EVIDENCE

When it's time to take down a dangerous suspect, SWAT teams get the job done. But before you can call in the troops, you've got to figure out who committed the crime. Forensic investigators look for tiny shreds of evidence that can lead them right to the criminal's front door.

Military breakthroughs in forensic science — developed to identify the casualities of war — help the police track down dangerous criminals. One high-tech tool civilian cops use is DNA fingerprinting.

Today's DNA technology was developed by the military, but not for fighting crime. They never wanted to bury another unknown soldier.

In preparation for Operation Desert Storm in 1990, the Department of Defense launched a program using DNA fingerprinting to identify GIs killed in action. They built a massive DNA "bank," collecting DNA samples from virtually every member of the armed forces.

But what if the fallen soldier you're trying to identify isn't in the DNA database? In the

SECRETS DECLASSIFIED

Deoxyribonucleic acid (DNA) is found in every human cell. We each have a unique DNA fingerprint. Forensic detectives find DNA in things such as saliva left on soda cans, a strand of hair, and blood or skin cells at a crime scene.

early 1990s, military scientists pioneered techniques to identify victims by matching their DNA to a surviving relative.

Using DNA technology, the military finally was able to identify the Vietnam War's unknown soldier in 1998. U.S. Air Force pilot Michael J. Blassie was moved from the Tomb of the Unknown Soldier to a cemetery near his family's home in St. Louis, Missouri.

LASER FINGERPRINTING

DNA fingerprinting wasn't the only forensic advance discovered by the military. In 1981, at the army's Criminal Investigation Lab in Atlanta, Georgia, Special Agent Ed German discovered a new laser fingerprinting technology.

Fingerprints aren't always visible to the naked

eye. German's technique involved treating the surface of an object with a chemical, then exposing it to a high-powered laser. Suddenly, fingerprints that were once invisible glowed before his eyes. One year later, Georgia police used the army's laser fingerprinting technique to put a murderer behind bars.

Forensic science's potential for the future is truly awesome. Someday police may be able to read the genetic code in DNA evidence to paint a picture of what a suspect looks like, helping both the police and the military lock up the bad guys.

NIGHT VISION

Tactical: Night vision gives the military critical sight in the dead of night.

Practical: Night vision blows away the criminal's cover of darkness.

Night vision allows the military to see what was once hidden — a humongous advantage if you're fighting an enemy in the dark. This amazing technology, developed over the past 50 years, has revolutionized reconnaissance and dominated the night battlefield.

The army's first attempts to see at night were at the end of World War II. Crude, bulky "sniper-scopes" allowed snipers to work at night, but they needed an infrared source to make them work. The whole idea was put aside because the devices were so big and hard to use, but it opened up the possibilities of night combat.

Then came the Korean War and the Battle for the Chosin Reservoir in 1952, when Communists attacked American troops in the dark. That attack led the army to expand its night-vision development.

Its new mission — to see and control the battlefield around the clock!

STARLIGHT SCOPE

The military set out to develop technology that would allow soldiers to fight as well at night as they did during the day. By the time of the Vietnam War, night-vision devices had been tested and perfected. Using the new Starlight Scope, soldiers could see the enemy's night moves.

Night-vision technology amplifies light, even when it looks like there isn't any! There's always light from somewhere — from the moon, the stars, or a city over the horizon. In 2003, that city was Baghdad.

United States and Coalition forces used the latest night-vision technology to shock the enemy under the cover of darkness in Operation Iraqi Freedom.

Now this technology is going mainstream! Police departments across the country have added night vision to their crime-fighting arsenal — blowing the cover off of nighttime crime.

?

Declassified Quiz:

Animal experts
use night-vision binoculars to
observe animals and their
nighttime adventures.
True or false?

Answer: True. At the Safari West animal preserve in Santa Rosa, California, information gained with night-vision technology may help save endangered species!

3

WIRED WARRIORS

In today's lightning-fast wars, the military needs to instantly deliver orders to soldiers who could be just about anywhere. And they've developed the technology to do the job.

That same advanced military technology has revolutionized the way the rest of us share information, talk to our friends, and even figure out where we are!

GLOBAL POSITIONING SYSTEM

Tactical: Global Positioning System, or GPS, pinpoints the enemy.

Practical: GPS helps drivers find their way.

Today, most luxury cars already have built-in GPS capable of identifying their exact location and displaying the best route to their destination.

Soon, not only will we know where the nearest fast-food restaurant is, we'll know how to get there using the least amount of fuel.

GPS, a space-based navigation tool, is the only system today that can show you your exact position on Earth — anytime, anywhere, in any weather. It is the single most advanced piece of military technology available to civilians.

Twenty-four GPS satellites — each with four atomic clocks — circle Earth twice a day at an altitude of 12,500 miles. These solar-powered satellites constantly adjust themselves in order to keep their solar panels toward the sun and their antennae toward Earth.

The satellites transmit time-code signals that can be

SECRETS DECLASSIFIED

GPS satellites are supported by a master control station at Falcon Air Force Base in Colorado Springs, Colorado, and by monitor stations around the world. They predict the behavior of each satellite's orbit and clock. This data is transmitted to the satellites, which communicate with the users, or receivers.

detected by anyone with a GPS receiver. When a receiver gets a signal from a satellite, it compares the time to its own internal clock and uses this to compute how far it is from the satellite. With four of these distances, from four different satellites, it pinpoints your latitude, longitude, altitude, and time!

CIVILIAN GPS

The first GPS satellites were rocketed into space in 1978. The full 24 GPS satellite constellation was orbiting Earth by 1994. Every branch of the military started figuring out ways to use it the minute the system became available, but it wasn't until 1983 that GPS was made available to civilians. Unfortunately, it took a major Cold War tragedy to make it happen.

On September 1, 1983, Korean Airlines Flight 007 accidentally wandered into Soviet Union airspace. The Soviets shot the plane down. All 269 passengers and crew members died.

GPS would have alerted the KAL pilots that their plane had wandered out of international airspace and into Soviet territory. After Flight 007,

SECRETS DECLASSIFIED

More than 95 miles of tunnel were dug below the English Channel to build the Channel Tunnel, or Chunnel.

President Ronald Reagan released GPS — which had been classified until then — to the civilian sector. GPS has had a major impact on every form of transportation ever since.

During the construction of a tunnel under the English Channel, British and French crews used GPS receivers to check their positions along the way. Since they were digging from opposite ends, they had to make sure they'd meet in the middle. If it wasn't for GPS, the tunnel might have been crooked.

GPS is also saving lives. Police, fire, and emergency medical service units use GPS receivers to determine which police car, fire truck, or ambulance is closest to an emergency, enabling the fastest possible response time in life-or-death situations. And search-and-rescue missions have used GPS to help find lost hikers and skiers in the mountains.

Declassified Quiz:

Tortoises in the Mojave Desert have been fitted with GPS receivers and tiny transmitters. True or false?

Answer: True! The transmitters help wildlife experts find out where the population is and determine possible sources of disease.

BATTLEFIELD TESTED

It wasn't until the Persian Gulf War in 1990 that GPS had its first battlefield test. Since the Gulf War was fought in the desert — a landscape without landmarks — GPS was essential in letting the military know where it was on the battlefield.

It wasn't just soldiers who found their way using GPS. So did bombs. When U.S. forces began shelling Baghdad in the spring of 2003, GPS-guided missiles and bombs hit their targets with surgical precision — able to pinpoint specific buildings on a block and even specific rooms within the building.

The future of GPS is limited only to our imaginations. Soon sophisticated surveillance robots will combine GPS with video capabilities to search for criminals and transmit their exact location to police officers!

WEAR GEAR

Tactical: High-tech gear keeps soldiers safe in battle and connected to their company.

Practical: High-tech gear gives athletes an edge in extreme sports.

Today's U.S. military uses the latest electronic technology and high-tech clothing to help soldiers fight stronger and longer.

SECRETS DECLASSIFIED

GPS has been getting more and more accurate ever since the first satellite was launched in the 1970s. In 1983, when there were only six GPS satellites, accuracy was about 200 yards. By 1995, 21 satellites had sharpened the accuracy to about 100 yards. Today, GPS can pinpoint a location within 10 yards or less!

WALKIE-TALKIES

World War II journalists gave the name walkie-talkie to the military's new two-way radios. They were portable and battery-operated. For the first time ever, battlefield commanders could talk to troops on the front lines.

Walkie-talkies were great for staying in touch over short distances, but the military wanted more. In 1973, the first handheld cellular phone was invented by an engineer named Martin Cooper. While even the best walkie-talkies have a range of about only 20 to 30 miles, the digital cell phone's range is much farther.

Unfortunately, cell phones can't be trusted for frontline communication because reception is unreliable and commands can be intercepted. In Afghanistan, one way the U.S. military tracked Al Qaeda terrorists was by pinpointing their locations during cell-phone calls.

SATELLITE PHONES

The military needed something better. So they came up with satellite phones!

Soldiers and vehicles deployed anywhere on the planet can be in touch, thanks to phones linked by military satellites. The latest encryption technology solves the interception problem and keeps sensitive communications secure. During Operation Iraqi Freedom, not only were the messages themselves encrypted but also the wavelength that they went over was scrambled. This double coding system makes it nearly impossible to break the code.

Satellite phones work anywhere, anytime. Using that same wireless technology, you could make a phone call or send an e-mail from the North Pole!

Now the military never has to ask the question, "Can you hear me now?"

BODY ARMOR

The military doesn't just have to worry about how to communicate with the troops no matter where they are, but also how to keep them safe in extreme environments.

Today's body armor is the result of a hundred years of testing in life-and-death conditions. In the 1970s, armor was revolutionized by jackets and helmets made of new types of fiber, such as Kevlar, that are lightweight and bulletproof.

The new generation of athletic safety equipment is like body armor for civilians. Specially padded football helmets use the same shock-absorbing material used on the decks of Navy SEAL boats, while mountain bikers and auto racers use body and head protection perfected by the military.

Sometimes, technology moves the other way, too. The soles of Special Forces combat boots are made from the same material that auto-racing tires use for traction.

EYEWEAR

Special Forces soldiers need more than high-tech clothing. The latest missiles and bombs use high-intensity lasers for guidance, so

today's military goggles and sunglasses don't just protect troops from blowing sand but also from potentially blinding laser light.

The military keeps its battle forces ready for anything with ultralight gear and the latest technology, offering lifesaving protection and critical communication.

COMPUTERS IN BATTLE — ONLINE AND ON TARGET

Tactical: Wireless technology keeps the U.S. military on the march.

Practical: Wireless technology gets us online from just about anywhere.

In the fog of war, anything can happen. Friendly

The Helios is the highest-flying UAV, reaching heights of 100,000 feet. It's lighter than a car and it's solar-powered!

© NICK GALANTE/AFP/Getty Images

© JUNG YEON-JE/AFP/Getty Images

THE HISTORY CHANNEL®

SWAT team members train for war. They work as a team and use civilian crime-fighting techniques to enforce the law.

The Spruce Goose was the largest seaplane ever built. Although never used in wartime, it was designed to carry 700 troops across the Atlantic.

© R. Eyerman/Time Life Pictures/Getty Images

© Reuters/Corbis

 The V-22 Osprey takes off and lands like a helicopter, but once in the air, it flies like an airplane.

GPS has become a civilian as well as a military tool, helping soldiers pinpoint the enemy's location, providing directions to a destination, and finding lost hikers and skiers in the mountains.

© AP Photo/NASA TV

Cameras are a basic tool for espionage. Models have become so small that they can be hidden in the palm of your hand.

© Jeffrey L. Rotman/CORBIS

High-tech gear and body armor help to keep soldiers safe and ready on the battlefield.

© David McNew/Getty Images

© Leif Skoogfors/CORBIS

 Dune buggies are lightweight off-road vehicles that can reach speeds of almost 140 miles per hour!

The Tomb of the Unknown Soldier in Arlington National Cemetery is guarded every hour of every day. It contains the remains of three unidentified soldiers from three different wars.

© Royalty–Free/CORBIS

© Spec. Robert Elliott/CORBIS

Humvees carry troops, supplies, and go anywhere a tank can. They're light enough to be transported by airplane and heavy enough to carry 5,900 pounds!

Night vision prevents the enemy from hiding in the dark. Now the battlefield can be monitored around the clock!

© Tim Wright/CORBIS

fire—a military situation in which soldiers are attacked in error by their own allies—is the most upsetting situation the military can face. During Operation Desert Storm in 1991, 35 soldiers were killed in friendly-fire incidents.

Enter Blue Force Tracking System. In the present Operation Iraqi Freedom, this wireless system gives frontline vehicles instant information as to who is a friend and who is an enemy. Blue for friendlies, red for the unknown.

SECRETS DECLASSIFIED

In the early 1960s, a professor at the Massachusetts Institute of Technology wrote down his ideas about a system of globally interconnected computers through which anyone could quickly access information from any site. The U.S. government funded research into what eventually became known as the Internet.

INTERNET TECHNOLOGY

Today's wired warrior is one part of a larger strategy — the U.S. forces want to know what's happening at all times.

The Internet and digital technology have not

only revolutionized the way we communicate (with cell phones, instant messaging, and e-mail), but also the way the military shares information.

In fast-paced modern warfare, wireless technology allows the military to deliver complicated orders almost instantaneously to just about anywhere.

Soon, soldiers will carry tracking systems in the palms of their hands, insuring that every foot soldier has a complete view of the battlefield.

DUDE, WHERE'S MY AMMO?

With troops using the latest technology to move faster, supply chains need to move just as quickly. In Operation Iraqi Freedom, some U.S. troops covered hundreds of miles in just a few days. Without supply chains following close behind, they'd be sitting ducks.

Sometimes, the most important information a commander can have is, "Where's my ammo? Where's my fuel?"

Radio frequency identification (RFID) answers those questions and more. RFID tracks all the supplies that the forces need using tiny microchips to store data and tiny antennae to transmit their exact location.

RFID is now being developed to keep track of supplies in civilian warehouses, too. Soon, every single product we

SECRETS DECLASSIFIED

RFID microchips are smaller than a grain of sand.

buy might have an RFID tag hidden inside. A store's warehouse will know to restock the shelf the minute you leave the store!

Privacy groups are campaigning to have RFID turned off at checkout, so no one can monitor how you're using their product after you get it home.

From the top command to the soldier in the trenches, the U.S. military is wired like never before. With military satellites and a tactical Internet, orders can be relayed around the world in an instant.

Wireless computing gives the rest of us instant access to the Internet from almost anywhere, but with it comes the threat of computer viruses and identity theft.

The race is on to develop advanced software protection for wireless networks. Who do you think will get there first — the military or a civilian?

4

TACTICAL WEAPONS, PRACTICAL APPLICATIONS

In the movies, bombs and weapons are all make-believe. Those huge explosions are cool to watch, right? But in the military, explosions are serious. Deadly serious.

Today, the U.S. military has an arsenal of weapons unmatched in human history. On the civilian side, that same technology not only entertains us but helps police fight the war on crime.

EXPLOSIVES

Tactical: Explosives are the most fearsome force in war.

Practical: Explosive force reshapes our world and amazes us with light and color.

When you think of explosives, you might think

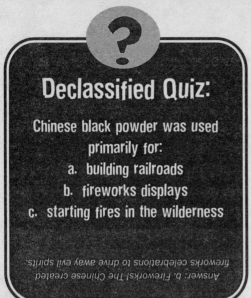

Declassified Quiz:

Chinese black powder was used primarily for:
a. building railroads
b. fireworks displays
c. starting fires in the wilderness

Answer: b. Fireworks! The Chinese created fireworks celebrations to drive away evil spirits.

of war, but explosives were not always used for battle. Black powder, the essential ingredient in early explosives, was invented by the Chinese in the eighth century. The use of black powder spread to Europe, and fireworks displays became increasingly elaborate.

In 1893, a man named Antonio Zambelli brought fireworks to the United States when he immigrated from Italy and established the Zambelli Fireworks Company in Pennsylvania.

Today, Zambelli Fireworks Internationale produces 4,000 fireworks shows a year — including 1,600 for the Fourth of July. More than one million fireworks shells are detonated around the country during the Fourth of July week alone.

NITROGLYCERIN

Fireworks weren't the only use for black powder — it wasn't long before it was used for gunpowder and war rockets as well. Then, in 1846, an Italian chemist discovered a much more explosive force — nitroglycerin.

Nitroglycerin was eight times more powerful than gunpowder, but it was very unstable. It went off with the smallest shock, and when it exploded, it took lives with it.

After a factory explosion killed his younger brother and four other people, Alfred Nobel (who also established the Nobel Prize) successfully developed a way to stabilize nitroglycerin in 1866. His invention — commonly known as dynamite — allowed explosives to be used more safely.

Dynamite was used almost immediately in the American West for mining and road and railroad construction. Before dynamite, tunnels had to be dug out with picks and shovels. With dynamite, when you came to a mountain, all you had to do was set a controlled blast and carry away the rubble!

MILITARY EXPLOSIVES

Alfred Nobel invented dynamite to make the world a safer place. He did not anticipate or desire its use by military forces around

SECRETS DECLASSIFIED

The first bombs dropped from airplanes were grenades. They had little effect, but led the way for bigger, more powerful aerial bombs.

the world as a brutal tool of war, but sure enough, the military found a use for dynamite as quickly as the railroads did.

Then, around the turn of the twentieth century, TNT (trinitrotoluene) was developed. TNT could be stored and handled even more safely than dynamite. Warfare changed forever.

World War I was mostly fought in the trenches, with soldiers shooting guns at one another. But the end of the war brought a new battle technique — aerial bombings. It was a preview of the terrifying tactics to come in World War II.

CARPET BOMBING

During World War II, the Allies developed carpet bombing. They used aircraft to carpet the ground with tons of bombs. It was a sophisticated technique for the time — made possible by the development of TNT — but the bombs could only hit within about a hundred yards of a target.

During the Vietnam War, public pressure grew to prevent the deaths of innocent civilians. The U.S. military developed video- and laser-guided systems for bombs. The accuracy rate skyrocketed. Vietnam-era bombs had an almost 90 percent hit ratio.

BUILDING DEMOLITION

The military isn't the only place where explosives have become more sophisticated. In today's crowded cities, when a building needs to come down, the demolition must be precise in order to avoid injuring people or damaging surrounding buildings. For these jobs the goal is implosion, not explosion. Specially shaped charges concentrate explosive force in one direction, so the building falls in on itself instead of exploding outward.

SMART BOMBS

Today's tactical bombs are guided by lasers and GPS in an even more strategic way — to an incredible 97 percent hit ratio.

By Operation Iraqi Freedom in 2003, smart bombs had been developed that could not only hit specific buildings with precision but even rooms within buildings. "Bunker Busters" — hardened bombs designed to pierce a structure and travel a preset distance before exploding — can even crash through reinforced concrete before detonation.

Even though accuracy has improved dramatically, there's no such thing as a fool-

SECRETS DECLASSIFIED

In 1993, 365 pounds of explosives, 300 special effects charges, and 460 gallons of aviation fuel were used to implode the Dunes Hotel in Las Vegas and to put on an amazing show. More than 250,000 people gathered to witness the Dunes' dazzling downfall — from a safe distance away, of course!

proof explosive. The next thing on the military's list? Developing "low-collateral" munitions — bombs that cause damage only to a specific area and leave the buildings and people around them unharmed.

WINNING THE WAR WITHOUT DEADLY FORCE

Tactical: Less lethal weapons allow the military to win wars with less deadly force.

Practical: Civilian police officers keep crime in check without endangering lives.

The goal of less lethal weapons is to stun, scare, sting, or immobilize — anything but kill. But they're not foolproof — that's why

SECRETS DECLASSIFIED

Flash Bangs, sting-balls, beanbag rounds, dazzlers, tasers, energy beams, and even sound waves are some of the less lethal weapons replacing gunfire today.

they're called less lethal, not nonlethal weapons.

LOW-IMPACT PROJECTILES

Beanbags, plastic pellets, and rubber batons are just a few of the "bullets" that can be fired from a pistol or a shotgun today. These low-impact projectiles strike a target with blunt force but don't usually kill.

Low-impact projectiles first came into use in Hong Kong, where British troops fired seven-inch wooden bullets against anticolonial protesters. The bullets were fired at the ground instead of directly at the protesters so that the bullets would skip off the ground and strike the protesters' legs. But some of the bullets bounced too high, causing serious injuries when they hit people in the face or the chest.

Soon bullets were made out of softer materials like rubber and plastic. But low-impact munitions don't work effectively on dangerous people who are high on drugs or alcohol. That's where tasers come in.

TASERS

The taser looks like a pistol, but it uses electric shock, rather than force, to incapacitate someone. Two electric darts, attached to a wire, are fired into an attacker. The wire transmits a 50,000-volt charge of electricity to stun but not to harm the person on the receiving end.

A gun that shoots electricity seems like something out of a science-fiction novel, and in a way, it is. Inventor

Jack Cover created the first high-voltage electrical gun in 1970. It was inspired by a series of books about a character named Tom Swift.

Taser is short for Tom Albert Swift Electrical Rifle. Like the gun in the children's book, the taser can knock a person down without serious injury.

Tasers have reduced injuries to suspects and to police officers around the country — and all because Jack Cover liked to read!

TEAR GAS

While tasers are effective in taking down one suspect, dealing with a large crowd requires other less lethal weapons.

In the Vietnam War, the U.S. military dropped tear gas over the jungle

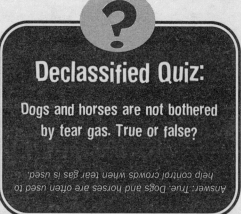

Declassified Quiz:

Dogs and horses are not bothered by tear gas. True or false?

Answer: True. Dogs and horses are often used to help control crowds when tear gas is used.

to unearth the enemy. At home, many people were protesting the same war. When the protests got out of hand, local police departments used surplus military tear gas to break up large crowds.

Tear gas makes your eyes burn and tear and causes coughing fits. It's a handy thing to have around if you have to break up a riot, but it has its drawbacks. Tear gas sends innocent bystanders into coughing fits just like rioters.

SECRETS DECLASSIFIED

Pepper spray is made from the hottest molecules on the planet.

PEPPER SPRAY

A new alternative to tear gas is pepper spray. The active ingredient in pepper spray comes from chili peppers. Like explosives, we got the idea from the Chinese. More than 2,000 years ago, Chinese warriors flung bags of red pepper at their enemies to stun them. Today, our delivery systems are a little better!

Pepper-ball launchers are similar to the guns used in paintball games, but the speed of these rounds is a lot higher. Soldiers and police officers can shoot up to six rounds per second.

Because the balls are shot with a pistol, they can be aimed at individual troublemakers instead of the whole crowd. And no one wants to be on the receiving end of one of these!

FLASH BANG

While pepper spray uses chemicals to subdue the bad guys, a new group of less lethal weapons stuns the enemy with flashes of blinding light, sound, or both.

The military is taking these weapons to a new level. New weapons can deploy intense light and sound beams — assaulting the enemy's vision and hearing.

Inventor Woody Norris is a pioneer of something called directional sound. A stereo speaker focuses sound into a tight beam, like a laser focuses light. Bombarding an enemy with high-pitched sound waves can make him dizzy, nauseous, and confused. It's kind of like sonic bullets.

SECRETS DECLASSIFIED

In 1990, when Panamanian dictator Manuel Noriega fled to the Vatican Embassy, U.S. Marines blasted him with 140-decibel heavy-metal music until he surrendered.

Soon, similar technology could be used in home theaters and cars. Step into the sound beam, and you'll hear loud and clear. Step out, and you'll hear nothing at all. Imagine being able to watch a movie in your living room while your sister blasts a CD just two feet away. And there won't be any more fighting over who controls the music in the car!

No one predicts an end to guns and grenades, but the development of less lethal weapons gives us new options in the wars against crime and terrorism — disabling the bad guys, while the good guys remain unharmed.

5

HIGH-MOBILITY VEHICLES

The United States military is a go-anywhere, do-anything fighting force. And they've developed some of the fastest, coolest, and toughest ways to get around on wheels. On the civilian side, that leads to fast and furious fun.

FROM HORSES TO HUMVEES

Tactical: The military Humvee is nearly unstoppable.

Practical: The civilian Hummer gives adventurers an awesome way to navigate the outdoors.

Its official military name is the High Mobility Multipurpose Wheeled Vehicle. Soldiers call it the Humvee. It can serve as a troop transport, an ambulance, a machine-gun platform, and even a missile launcher. You may have seen one of its civilian cousins in your own neighborhood and wondered, "Where did that thing come from?"

It's a war story.

A TANK OF A CAR

During World War I and into the 1930s, the U.S. Army's High Mobility Multipurpose Vehicle had one horsepower — four-hoof drive.

Then came the Jeep. The Jeep combined the ruggedness of a truck with the speed and mobility of a light car — and it was easier to take care of than a horse. The Jeep was mass produced for U.S. forces beginning in 1940, and it was the vehicle used to move troops in World War II and Vietnam. But it had some problems.

Not only was the Jeep limited in the number of troops and supplies it could carry, certain models had a deadly tendency to roll over.

So the army went back to the drawing board. In the late 1970s, they developed the requirements for a new wheeled vehicle. It had to be highly mobile, multipurpose, and go anywhere an M-1 tank could go. It took 10 months to build the first prototype.

SECRETS DECLASSIFIED

The Jeep's name comes from the abbreviation for "general purpose" (g.p.) vehicle.

57

After 600,000 miles of driving over rocky hills and valleys, in deep sand and mud, in desert heat and Arctic cold, the Humvee passed every test with flying colors. Not only was it highly mobile and multipurpose, it was light enough to be delivered to any hot spot by air. Since 1983, more than 150,000 Humvees have been delivered to the military.

THE HUMMER

When watching the Humvee race across the desert in the Persian Gulf War, civilians learned what military drivers had known for years — the Humvee rules! And they wanted to get in on the action.

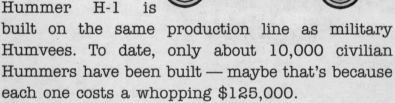

The civilian Hummer H-1 is built on the same production line as military Humvees. To date, only about 10,000 civilian Hummers have been built — maybe that's because each one costs a whopping $125,000.

The H-1 and the new H-2 have fancy extras the military Humvee doesn't — things like air conditioning, soundproofing, and stereos.

The civilian Hummer may have become more

comfortable, but the military Humvee has gotten a lot tougher.

UP–ARMORED

The original Humvee weighed about 5,200 pounds and could carry a payload of 2,500 pounds. Today's more rugged Humvee weighs only 700 pounds more, but can carry 5,900 pounds — more than double the payload.

With a greater payload, not only can the Humvee carry more troops and supplies, but it also can be armored against battlefield threats.

Declassified Quiz:

Which movie star ordered the first civilian Hummer in 1991?

a. Ben Affleck
b. Arnold Schwarzenegger
c. Will Smith

Answer: b. Arnold Schwarzenegger, aka the Terminator and now the governor of California.

SECRETS DECLASSIFIED

Payload is the quantity of cargo (load) that a plane, train, car, or other vehicle can carry.

The up-armored Humvee got its ultimate test in 1997. In Bosnia, three U.S. MPs ran over a 14-pound antitank mine. It shattered their Humvee's engine and blew off a wheel, but all three MPs walked away unhurt.

Today's military rides an even faster, tougher, and safer Humvee. The High Mobility Multipurpose Wheeled Vehicle will continue to be a fearsome fighting force well into the twenty-first century.

SMARTTRUCK

So far there's no replacement for the Humvee, but there is a challenger and it's called the SmartTruck. Buckle your seat belt, because this truck has features that would make even James Bond jealous. In fact, the military's designers got some of their ideas from James Bond movies!

If the Humvee is the ultimate off-road vehicle, the SmartTruck will be the ultimate in-city ride. It's built for protection in dangerous urban environments.

SECRETS DECLASSIFIED

The Marines adapted the Humvee to drive in up to five feet of water. NASA's MARS-1 Humvee Rover has successfully crossed the Wellington Channel, a 23-mile stretch of treacherous sea ice in the Canadian High Arctic, and may one day be used on the red planet it's named after.

The SmartTruck began as a standard Ford heavy-duty pickup, but that's the only standard thing about it. Its on-board computer system — voice and touch-activated — controls all truck navigation and defense. Features like blinding lights, oil sprays, and bomb-detection equipment are all still in the demo phase, but the SmartTruck is a prototype for the future.

And who knows, maybe one day you'll see one driving through your neighborhood, declassified for civilian use.

ALL-TERRAIN VEHICLES (ATVS)

Tactical: Off-road, lightweight military vehicles bring speed and firepower to the battlefield.

Practical: Dune buggies take anyone anywhere, anytime!

When it comes to ATVs, it's a case of the practical leading the tactical. This is one area where civilian technology beats the military. Desert off-road races in places like Baja, Mexico, have pushed ATV technology to the limit. Now, Navy

Seals use the same technology to meet the enemy on their own ground.

DUNE BUGGIES

Nothing tests the strength and endurance of an off-road vehicle like the rugged desert terrain of Baja, Mexico. Engineer and artist Bruce Myers drove the first dune buggy, nicknamed "Old Red," the length of Baja in 1967. Myers drove from La Paz to Tijuana in only 34 hours — shattering the motorcycle record by five hours.

Along the way, he started the dune-buggy craze and created the sport of desert off-road racing. Today's desert racers rip across the desert at speeds of almost 140 miles per hour. And today's drivers have equipped their buggies with GPS to guide them across desert wastelands.

The sport was born in the deserts of Baja, but the dune buggy traces its roots to the battlefields of World War II.

KUBELWAGON

Ferdinand Porsche created the Volkswagen Kubelwagon for Hitler's army as a go-anywhere vehicle to rival the American Jeep. It was a thousand pounds lighter than the Jeep, weighing in at only 1,700 pounds. But the biggest difference between the Kubelwagon and the Jeep wasn't its size, it was where Porsche put the engine — in the back.

Even though the Kubelwagon was only two-wheel drive, its rear engine gave it enough power and traction to drive over heavy sand or snow. It skipped over rough terrain using agility rather than brute force, and it got twice the gas mileage of the jeep. American forces loved driving around in captured German Kubelwagons just like they would one day love dune buggies.

DESERT PATROL VEHICLES

Dune-buggy rides can be a thrill, but for Special Ops teams, tours in the deserts of the Middle East are serious and demand serious vehicles.

Navy Seals modified the ATV to create the Desert Patrol Vehicle. DPVs may not have the power of a Humvee, but they're almost impossible to catch. They get in quick, do the job, and get out fast. With a range of more than 600 miles, the DPV can penetrate deep into enemy territory to recover downed pilots or scout enemy positions.

In 1991's Operation Desert Storm, the DPV faced its first battlefield test. The first U.S. forces to enter Kuwait City on the day it was liberated rolled in on DPVs. They raced ahead of other U.S. troops to scout out territory and darted behind enemy lines to scope out the size and position of enemy forces.

ATTACK VEHICLES

The DPV is an amazing off-road tool for the military, but the future of military off-road vehicles may be the Advanced Light Strike Vehicle (ALSV). This four-wheel-drive attack car will muscle over any kind of terrain. It's designed to penetrate, survive, and win on the high-intensity battlefield of the future.

The ALSV has a gunner seat that can rotate 360 degrees. It can carry a 50-caliber machine

SECRETS DECLASSIFIED

The first DPVs had Volkswagen engines. Today they have Porsche engines and go as fast as 70 to 75 miles per hour. Iraqi soldiers call them "ninja cars."

gun or an automatic grenade launcher. In the Persian Gulf War, the ALSV operated undetected deep behind enemy lines, performing reconnaissance and missions for the U.S. Marine Corps and the U.S. Navy SEALs.

Future military ATVs might not even have drivers. The army is experimenting with radio-controlled ATVs that can scout enemy positions, search for land mines, and even conduct rescue missions under enemy fire.

HUMAN-POWERED ATVS

You may not think a mountain bike has a tactical application, but the military has been riding bikes for over a hundred years.

In 1896, buffalo soldiers of the Twenty-Fifth Bicycle Corps tested the bicycle by riding more than 1,900 miles from Missoula, Montana, to St. Louis, Missouri. And they didn't use one road — it was all rough terrain.

Today, the military is still using bikes. The

Declassified Quiz:

A paratrooper is:
a. a foot soldier
b. a soldier trained to parachute into enemy territory
c. a civilian who temporarily does a soldier's job

Answer: b. Paratroopers jump right into the action — from airplanes, of course!

army is testing a foldable mountain bike for its paratroopers. The bike is tough enough to be tossed out of an airplane, durable enough to handle any terrain, and fast enough to move at high speeds. Soon, it may be supplied to all the army's airborne troops.

From dune buggies to bikes, lightweight off-road vehicles give the military a fast and furious way to get across rough terrain. At the same time, these vehicles give civilians a fun way of exploring deserts, mountains, and everything in between. From practical to tactical and back to practical again!

DECLASSIFIED CHALLENGE

Now that you've read all about these cool military inventions and their uses in everyday life, see if you have what it takes to serve with the best military force in the world!

1. The Kettering Bug was the first:
a. military dune buggy
b. reconnaissance UAV
c. cruise missile

2. The CIA was created during which war?
a. the Civil War
b. the Cold War
c. the Vietnam War

3. GPS stands for:
a. Global Positioning Satellite
b. Guided Paratrooper System
c. Global Paramilitary Service

4. Who invented dynamite?

a. Howard Hughes

b. Alfred Nobel

c. Glenn Curtiss

5. The military's high-mobility vehicle in World War I was:

a. the bicycle

b. the jeep

c. the horse

6. What is "Snake" the nickname for?

a. the Marines' Super Cobra helicopter

b. the Navy SEALs' first DPV

c. a CIA secret weapon

7. Which battle led the military to develop high-tech night vision?

a. the Battle of Midway in World War II

b. Vietnam's Tet Offensive

c. the Battle for the Choisin Reservoir in the Korean War

8. Why doesn't the U.S. military use digital cell phones?

a. Cell phone signals can be intercepted by the enemy.

b. You can't always get reception.

c. both

9. Which of these weapons was named for the inventor's favorite science fiction novel?

a. the Taser

b. beanbag bullets

c. pepper spray

10. SmartTruck's features were inspired by which famous fictional spy?

a. Agent Cody Banks

b. James Bond

c. the Spy Kids

ANSWERS TO DECLASSIFIED CHALLENGE

1.c 2.b 3.a 4.b 5.c 6.a 7.c 8.c 9.a 10.b

SCORECARD:

If you answered 8 or more questions correctly, you're one of today's Super Warriors! You have the high-tech tools it takes to penetrate enemy lines and live to tell the tale!

If you answered between 5 and 7 questions correctly, you need to upgrade your declassified secrets. In a battle between you and the enemy, the enemy just might win!

If you answered 4 or fewer questions correctly, go back to basic training! Seriously, it's time to bone up on your military know-how!